COCA-COLA MEMORABILIA

THE COLLECTOR'S CORNER

COCA-COLA MEMORABILIA

TODTRI

A QUANTUM BOOK

Published in the United States by
TODTRI Book Publishers
254 West 31st Street
New York, NY 10001-2813
Fax: (212) 695-6984
E-mail: info@todtri.com

Visit us on the web!
www.todtri.com

ISBN 1-57717-211-6

QUMCCMM

This book is produced by
Quantum Publishing Ltd
6 Blundell Street
London N7 9BH

Printed in Singapore by Star Standard Industries (Pte) Ltd

CONTENTS

COCA-COLA COLLECTABLES

● ● ● ●

ABOVE. This sign from 1942 was made of paper stretched over a metal disk.

Coca-Cola has been a part of American life for more than a century. From its humble beginnings in 1886 in Atlanta, Georgia, to its current status as the world's best-known soft drink, Coca-Cola has always been heavily advertised. Millions of promotional items have been produced to advertise and sell the product. These promotional products have ranged from utilitarian merchandising such as bottles and coolers to more traditional and familiar advertising in the form of signs and magazine advertisements; from point-of-purchase items such as trays, clocks and calendars to novelties such as watches, penknives, toys, games and bookmarks.

These are the articles that form the basis for today's collections, part of their attraction being that they were originally made to promote sales, not to be collected. There are three main factors in the evaluation of a Coca-Cola collectable: rarity, condition and desirability.

RIGHT This cardboard cutout sign from 1929 is the centerpiece of the five-piece "Nasturtium" festoon. It was used at soda fountains.

Drink **Coca-Cola**
Delicious and Refreshing

quality materials — it cost $5,000 just for the dies needed to produce a self-framed metal sign featuring "Betty," the Coca-Cola girl for 1914. The items were also attractive, ensuring that people saved them at the time.

Due to the huge interest in collecting older pieces of memorabilia, new pieces are now created for the collectors' market. The company was originally against this, but through licensing agreements with various manufacturers, it now helps to identify images and items that may be produced for sale.

New items using old artwork fall into two categories: those that closely imitate old items are called reproductions, and those that do not are called fantasy items. Since many of these new pieces appear older than they actually are, collectors not only have to be knowledgeable about older items, but also about the reproduction and fantasy items on the market.

As The Coca-Cola Company expanded to reach more than 195 countries around the world, they have tailored the advertising approach to suit

LEFT This sign was printed in the United States, for export to The Netherlands. It dates from 1947.

BELOW This 1900 metal tray features "Hilda Gray with a Glass." The border is decorated with cola nuts and coca leaves.

Coca-Cola collectables span the full range of artifacts manufactured to merchandise and advertise consumer products since the 1880s. In retrospect, The Coca-Cola Company was not a merchandising and advertising genius. It simply used all means available and was unusual in its aggressive advertising throughout the good and the bad times.

There are a number of reasons for the survival of so many Coca-Cola collectables today. Huge numbers of different articles were made, and usually of the best-

7

individual countries. The result has been a whole new area of collectables, with Coca-Cola advertising appearing in a multitude of languages. Pieces which are unique to a country, rather than just imitating the advertising used in the United States, are especially prized by collectors.

Although it is now a truly international product, Coca-Cola is regarded worldwide as an icon of American life. Coca-Cola collectables hold a mirror to America's past and present: its customs, values, tastes, obsessions, pleasures, and troubles.

LEFT The boy vendor in this artwork would have been a familiar sight at ballparks in the 1920s. A nearly-life sized version was also made.

BELOW This sign is one of the largest metal indoor Coca-Cola signs made. The "Betty" artwork was used on 1914 calendars.

CHAPTER ONE

THE COCA-COLA STORY

• • • •

C oca-Cola is said to have been created in 1886 by a Dr. John S. Pemberton. He had already marketed many products, one of which was "French Wine Coca," containing wine and extract of coca. By 1886, possibly due to the anti-alcohol movement, Pemberton decided to make a non-alcoholic product based on French Wine Coca. To disguise the unpleasant taste of this mixture of coca and kola (taken from a West African nut), he added aromatic oils and spices; including orange, vanilla, nutmeg, coriander and cinnamon. This product was then sold as a medicine to be taken "a teaspoonful in a glass of water." Pemberton soon decided to use carbonated water as the mixer.

ABOVE When Coca-Cola syrup and carbonated water had been poured into a glass, this spoon would have been used to mix the finished product.

LEFT By 1907, the Coca-Cola company had branches throughout the United States, Canada and Cuba, as shown on this letterhead.

Credit for the name "Coca-Cola" is usually given to Frank M. Robinson, secretary of the Pemberton Chemical Company. By changing the "k" in kola to a "c," Robinson was following the trend of using alliterative names for products in the drug trade. Robinson is also credited with designing the distinctive script form of the name.

Asa G. Candler, a fellow druggist, was interested in the company because he had tried the product, with some success, as a cure for his headaches. He gained control of Coca-Cola from Pemberton in 1888. He then hired Robinson as general superintendent, and changed the formula so that Coca-Cola syrup would be more uniform, chemically stable, and better tasting. Sales of Coca-Cola increased from twenty-five gallons in 1886 to 8,855 gallons in 1890. Collectables from this period are extremely rare – and mostly consist of letters written by Pemberton, Candler, and others within the company on the distinctive "Coca-Cola" stationery.

RIGHT Coca-Cola-flavored chewing gum was made from 1903 until the 1920s, at first in Atlanta and later in Richmond, Virginia.

On April 13, 1891, Candler became the sole proprietor of Coca-Cola. By 1895, he was able to report that "Coca-Cola is now sold and drunk in every state and territory in the United States."

DRINK BOTTLED
Coca-Cola
Delightfully Carbonated
and
So Easily Served

The 1890s would see the first expansion of syrup-making facilities to locations outside Atlanta and the first bottling of the finished product (Coca-Cola plus carbonated water). A system of syrup wholesalers, called "parent bottlers," was later established to act as middlemen between The Coca-Cola Company and the local bottlers.

Advertising and sales

From the beginning The Coca-Cola Company understood the connection between advertising and sales and the product was advertised heavily. Annual percentage comparisons were made between the increased amount spent on advertising and the increased sales of Coca-Cola.

From the late 1890s into the 1910s, Wolf & Company arranged much of the advertising for Coca-Cola. The Massengale Agency was responsible for placing advertisements for Coca-Cola in the early part of this century. William C. D'Arcy was selected in 1906 to help place advertising, and by the end of the decade, was handling more than a quarter of the advertising budget. The bottling business also thrived, and increasingly, advertising depicted Coca-Cola in bottles.

Seeing off the competition

As a result of its success, The Coca-Cola Company was the target of imitators. Prosecutions were filed against the Koke Company, Karo-Cola, Curo-Cola, Koca-Nola, and Taka-Kola. Some Coca-Cola enthusiasts also collect the imitators' advertising, though they are worth relatively little.

The Pure Food and Drug Act in 1906 meant that Coca-Cola also became the target of litigation concerning its contents, especially the caffeine. In 1917, as the United States found itself involved in World War I and sugar rationing began, the company was forced to curtail the production of syrup. Advertising was kept to a minimum, since there was no point in advertising a product with limited supply. Coca-Cola sales dropped, but with the end of the war and the easing of restrictions, sugar became available again, advertising increased, and, by 1919, sales were better than in 1917.

LEFT This free-drink coupon, letter, and envelope date from about 1895. The strategy of mailing coupons for free drinks to potential customers was largely responsible for the early success of Coca-Cola.

BELOW The upper portion of this ceramic urn held Coca-Cola syrup that was dispensed directly into a glass. The urn dates from about 1900.

CARDBOARD CUTOUTS

Among the most collectable of Coca-Cola memorabilia are the cardboard cutouts. These can be used not only to trace the development of the company, but also the changing trends in American life. The subjects covered and the styles of artwork alter over time according to fashion and current events. The company employed some of the foremost illustrators of the day, making the cutouts valuable for their artistic merit as well as their content.

LEFT The new larger size Coca-Cola glass is introduced on this cardboard cutout. The display also portrays America's love affair with the automobile.

RIGHT The Sprite was first seen in Coca-Cola advertising in 1942 when he was used to familiarize customers with the word "Coke." He was used again later to introduce larger bottles.

Have a LARGE Coke...

BELOW Ventriloquist Edgar Bergen and his dummy Charlie McCarthy were sponsored by the Coca-Cola Company to appear on the CBS radio network from 1949 to 1952.

Coca-Cola *brings you*
Edgar Bergen *with*
Charlie McCarthy
CBS SUNDAY EVENINGS
DRINK Coca-Cola

Changing hands

The trademark infringement case brought against the Koke Company in 1912 was not yet settled in 1919 when a consortium of banks offered $25 million to purchase The Coca-Cola Company. Fearing the loss of the Coca-Cola trademark and tiring of endless lawsuits, the stockholders accepted the offer and the business was reincorporated as a publicly-held Delaware corporation. The name, The Coca-Cola Company, stayed the same. The Koke Company case was resolved in The Coca-Cola Company's favor in 1920.

Although sales rebounded to an all-time high in 1919, they decreased from 1920 to 1922. The new owners of the company were concerned and in 1923, elected Robert Woodruff president of the company. He established

a Quality Control Department, reorganized the Sales Department, and increased the salesmen's role to include responsibility for placing advertising correctly. Sales increased in 1923 and every year thereafter.

Coca-Cola had been sold outside the United States before Woodruff's presidency, but only on a relatively disorganized basis. In 1923, he set up a separate division for establishing bottling plants overseas, and by 1929 there were Coca-Cola bottlers in 29 countries.

The first six-bottle carton was introduced in 1923 and the first standardized cooler for bottled Coca-Cola in 1929. Two new advertising media were added during the decade, in the form of 24-sheet billboards and radio programs. Many of the famous Coca-Cola slogans began in the 1920s, such as: "Thirst knows no season," "Enjoy thirst,"

ABOVE The Startup Candy Company manufactured "chocolate pellets filled with Coca-Cola syrup" which were sold in cardboard boxes.

ABOVE The familiar trademark "Coca-Cola" marked on the bottle top was one of the ways of identifying the early crown-top Coca-Cola bottles.

LEFT Coca-Cola was shipped in wooden barrels such as this one from the 1890s until World War II. This particular barrel dates from 1939.

13

"Refresh yourself," "It had to be good to get where it is," "Pure as sunlight," and "The pause that refreshes."

Despite the Great Depression, The Coca-Cola Company continued to grow throughout the 1930s. A parallel can be drawn to Hollywood's success over this period, and the escapism that the movies provided was capitalized upon by Coca-Cola. Numerous movie stars, including Joan Crawford, Clark Gable, Cary Grant, Jean Harlow, and Loretta Young, were used in Coca-Cola advertising.

BELOW This full-page advertisement appeared in the American Weekly section of Sunday newspapers on June 14, 1936.

The automatic fountain dispenser for Coca-Cola was introduced in 1933. The first commercially successful coin-operated coolers were developed in the mid-1930s. Metal one-gallon syrup cans were first used to ship syrup in 1939. *The Coca-Cola Radio Program* had its debut in 1930; Haddon Sundblom's Coca-Cola Santas began to appear in 1931; the *When You Entertain* campaign was inaugurated in 1932; and famous illustrators – Norman Rockwell, Frederick Stanley and N. C. Wyeth – created the

SERVICE ABOVE SELF

Be a Lifesaver — Buy War Bonds and Stamps
Armed only with courage, and dedicated to saving life and relieving pain, the men of the Medical Department go into battle. Where shells scream and bullets whine these men perform their duty. A minute saved may mean a life saved. Beside the men who fall they serve, giving first aid, quenching thirst, guarding until stretchers come. Theirs is a true devotion to mercy, a Service Above Self!

1943		**October**			**1943**	
SUNDAY	MONDAY	TUESDAY	WEDNESDAY	THURSDAY	FRIDAY	SATURDAY
					1	**2**
3	**4**	**5**	**6**	**7**	**8**	**9**
10	**11**	**12**	**13**	**14**	**15**	**16**
17	**18**	**19**	**20**	**21**	**22**	**23**
24 31	**25**	**26**	**27**	**28**	**29**	**30**

DELICIOUS *Coca-Cola* REFRESHING
THE COCA-COLA BOTTLING WORKS COMPANY

ABOVE Coca-Cola bottlers distributed this calendar through a project called "Schools at War." It encouraged children to save their money for the war effort. The artwork shows a medic giving aid to a wounded soldier on the battlefront.

distinctive Coca-Cola artwork between 1931 and 1937. Two more radio programs debuted during the 1930s: *Refreshment Time* and *The Song Shop*.

World War II

During World War II Woodruff directed that, "We will see that every man in uniform gets a bottle of Coca-Cola for five cents wherever he is and whatever it costs." The company built bottling plants overseas and eventually 64 plants were built in North Africa, Europe, Australia, and the Philippines.

The war was the predominant advertising theme at this time: men and women in uniform, ships and planes. Game kits containing bingo, dominoes, checkers, darts and ping-pong were distributed to military bases. Coca-Cola also capitalized on the contract bridge craze of the time; marking decks of playing cards, score sheets, and even tables and chairs with the Coca-Cola logo. The annual advertising budget doubled from 1941 to 1948. Having lost a trademark infringement case against Pepsi-Cola, the trade-mark notification was now centered below the word "Coca-Cola" instead of appearing in the first "C" in "Coca" — a change that helps collectors to date merchandise. In 1941, the company started using the name "Coke" and registered this as a trademark in 1945.

In July 1944, the one-billionth gallon of Coca-Cola syrup was manufactured. During the 1950s the price of a drink of Coca-Cola finally exceeded 5¢. In 1955 a range of bottles were introduced, in ten-ounce, 12-ounce, and 26-ounce sizes. A 12-ounce glass was also produced, and "pre-mix" vending machines were introduced. The flat-top can was first used during the 1950s.

Television

Advertising for Coca-Cola entered the television era in 1950 with a Thanksgiving Day special. The company's second show, a Christmas special later that same year, also marked Walt Disney's first entry into television. Later on in the decade, Coca-Cola went on to sponsor the television programs *Coke Time* with Eddie Fisher, *The Mickey Mouse Club*, and *The Adventures of Kit Carson*.

LEFT In the 1940s, the company gave in to pressure to use the name "Coke." This plastic bottle topper demonstrates this change of heart.

BELOW The "Buddy Lee" doll wearing Coca-Cola uniform was first sold to the public in the 1950s.

New connections

The Coca-Cola Company's fifty-year association with the D'Arcy Advertising Company ended in 1956. A new firm – McCannErickson – took over responsibility for promoting Coca-Cola.

The first new logo since the bull's-eye logo debuted in 1958. Officially known as the "archiform" or "fishtail", it was abandoned in the early 1960s.

BELOW "Space Cans" went up on the Challenger space shuttle, making Coke the first carbonated drink to be drunk in space.

Two of the most popular advertising items for Coca-Cola appeared in the 1950s: the Buddy Lee doll (1950) and the Santa Claus doll (1955).

New products

The Coca-Cola Company departed from its one-product rule in the 1950s with the introduction of the Fanta line. Sprite, TAB, Fresca, and Simba followed in the 1960s.

New promotions

During the 1960s singers such as the Supremes, Neil Diamond, Ray Charles, and Aretha Franklin were recruited to promote Coca-Cola. The "things go better with Coke" logo and slogan were first seen in 1963. In 1966, the new "harlequin" or checkerboard can design appeared. A new slogan, "It's the real

ENJOY

CENTENNIAL CELEBRATION

ABOVE The Coca-Cola Company celebrated its 100th anniversary during the week of May 8, 1986. The special logo designed for the centennial celebration is shown at the bottom of this paper poster.

thing" and new logo, the "Arden Square" with the "dynamic ribbon device" appeared in 1969.

In 1971 "I'd like to teach the world to sing…" sold over a million copies. In 1979 the Pittsburgh Steelers' "Mean" Joe Greene appeared in a Coca-Cola TV commercial. The 1980s saw the creation of "megabrand" Coca-Cola: diet Coke, caffeine-free Coke, Cherry Coke, "new" Coke, and Classic Coca-Cola. In 1985 specially designed Coca-Cola. cans went up in the Space Shuttle. Coca-Cola celebrated its hundredth anniversary in 1986.

CHAPTER TWO

ADVERTS AND CALENDARS

• • • •

Advertisements in newspapers and magazines were the earliest form of mass media used to advertise Coca-Cola. Because advertising and articles in periodicals have been produced regularly from Coca-Cola's beginnings, they are a rich source of collectables and of information about Coca-Cola. Because of the reasonable price of periodical advertising, even novice collectors are able to accumulate an impressive collection of original newspaper and magazine advertisements. However, collectors must be cautious, because unscrupulous individuals can produce color photocopies that are quite difficult to tell from the originals.

Coca-Cola was first advertised in *The Daily Journal* newspaper in Atlanta on

May 29, 1886. The now familiar script Coca-Cola trademark had not been created at this time, and "Coca-Cola" appeared in plain block letters. The advertisement read: "Coca-Cola, Delicious, Refreshing, Exhilarating, Invigorating, The New and Popular Soda Fountain Drink, containing the properties of the wonderful Coca plant and the famous Cola nuts. For sale by Willis Venable and Nunnally &

All over the world... Sign of Good Taste... In ever-widening circles, the uniquely pleasant taste of Coca-Cola wins fresh appreciation and new friends. Through more than 100 countries today...more than 58 million times each day...someone enjoys the special flavor, the welcome little lift, of Coke. This remarkable endorsement has won for Coca-Cola a gracious badge of good taste; that's all its own...recognized everywhere. There's just no substitute for Coke, best-loved sparkling drink in all the world.

Coca-Cola SIGN OF GOOD TASTE

Thirst knows no season

Drink **Coca-Cola**

5¢

The Coca-Cola Company
Atlanta, Ga.

Rawson." In more than a dozen ads in 1886, Coca-Cola appeared in block letters. The first known use of script Coca-Cola appeared in *The Daily Journal* on June 16, 1887. It read simply, "Coca-Cola, Delicious, Refreshing, Exhilarating, Invigorating." The phrase "Coca-Cola, Delicious, Refreshing" has continued to be the most used phrase in its advertising.

Trade publications

Beginning in the 1890s, Coca-Cola was promoted in trade publications published for owners and employees of drug stores and soda fountains. These advertisements often told of the profit that could be made by selling Coca-Cola. Around the turn of the century, trade pub-

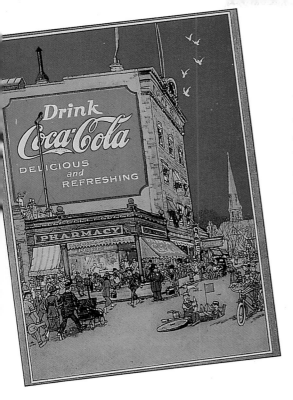

The artwork used was original and often full color. It changed every year, making magazine advertisements depicting every phase of American life, one of the most fascinating areas of collecting. During this same period, newspaper advertising also flourished. Some newspaper ads used the same artwork as magazines, while others advertised local events along with the name, location, and phone number of the local bottler.

Local publications

In addition to advertising in magazines and newspapers, The Coca-Cola Company and local bottlers began to advertise in local publications such as telephone and city directories, high school and college annuals, church bulletins, and programs for theaters, circuses, and athletic events. Most of these employed artwork not used elsewhere. The Coca-Cola Company also published periodicals and one-time publications for the general public. Household entertaining and decorating hints were featured in the *When You Entertain* book, the *Flower Arranging* books, and the *Pause for Living* booklets.

lications for the advertising business began to appear. Articles on advertising campaigns used by The Coca-Cola Company were often included. Sign and novelty manufacturers placed full-color advertisements showcasing the Coca-Cola items they had produced.

Consumer magazines

The Coca-Cola Company first placed advertisements in national consumer magazines in 1904. The same ad was placed in six nationally distributed magazines. This advertisement featured the 1903 Coca-Cola calendar girl, and read, "Drink Coca-Cola at Soda Fountains and Carbonated in Bottles 5¢." From 1905 to 1907, magazine advertising blossomed.

When the Sun is Red Hot and you and your collar are limp as rags; when your mouth and throat are the only dry spots on you and you are very, very thirsty, there's just one thing to do—

Drink

Coca-Cola

It will freshen you up—please your palate and quench your thirst as no other liquid will.

Delicious——Refreshing——Wholesome Thirst-Quenching

GET THE GENUINE

5c Everywhere

Company publications

Starting in 1896, another category of monthly periodical, this time for people in the Coca-Cola business, began with the introduction of *The Coca-Cola News* in Seth W. Fowle's New England territory. *The Coca-Cola Bottler* magazine began in 1909 for employees of local bottlers. In 1921, *The Friendly Hand* newsletter started for employees of The Coca-Cola Company. This was superseded in 1924 by *The Red Barrel* magazine, which was distributed to a broader audience, including soda fountain operators and bottler employees.

In 1948, *Coca-Cola Overseas* debuted and contained stories, as the name suggests, about Coca-Cola sales operations outside the United States. In 1953, *The Red Barrel* ceased publication with the introduction of *Refresher* magazine. These publications have pictures of the advertising available, articles about improving sales of Coca-Cola, stories about Coca-Cola employees, and general company news.

Coca-Cola calendars

The earliest known Coca-Cola calendar dates from 1891. Starting in the mid-1890s, the artwork used on the Coca-Cola calendar was also used on other advertising of the same year. Fortunately for collectors, The Coca-Cola Company used this advertising strategy well into the 1950s, and it is especially helpful for dating items that have the same artwork as that year's calendar.

It is now generally agreed among collectors that the date that should be associated with a collectable is its year of first use as established by the artwork on the annual Coca-Cola calendar. This rule stands even though the item itself may show a copyright date from an earlier year.

In 1904, the company and parent bottlers began issuing different calendars each year, one dedicated to fountain sales and the other to the sale of Coca-Cola in bottles.

In addition to company-issued calendars, some local Coca-Cola bottlers produced their own calendars as early as the 1930s. These featured stock artwork (not prepared specially for Coca-Cola) showing such things as landscapes, wildlife, and Boy Scouts. Since these calendars were distributed to businesses and homes within the local bottler's territory, they were imprinted with the bottler's name, address, and telephone number.

LEFT The "archiform" logo on this calendar display was not used after 1963. This item probably lasted until well after that date, however.

Calendars overseas

The company also produced calendars for foreign markets. Examples from the 1930s and 1940s generally used the indigenous languages, but carried the same artwork as used on American advertising items. Slight modifications were sometimes made to the artwork, such as changing blonde hair to brunette for Latin American countries. Examples from the 1950s typically portray the language, people, and culture of the country where the calendar was distributed.

BELOW This high-quality bronze desk calendar was used with durable plastic date cards that could be swapped according to the month and year.

In most instances, the very same artwork was used on both calendars, but one version showed a glass of Coca-Cola, while the other showed a bottle. In some years, entirely different artwork was used for the two versions. The last calendars to be handled in this way were those made for 1927. The practice of having bottle versus glass variations on other items, however, continued on into the 1940s.

21

Until 1940 the calendars in the United States consisted of a single artwork which was visible for the year. After that, calendars used at least six pages, each with a different artwork and a calendar for two months. Most were intended to be displayed where Coca-Cola was sold. In 1954, The Coca-Cola Company introduced the "home calendar," sent directly to customers' homes. Also called reference calendars, they carried useful information such as holiday dates. From the 1960s, smaller business calendars called "calendar displays" were distributed. They consisted of a metal back plate, which carried the

Compliments of
D. H. WALLACE PHARMACY
VEEDERSBURG,   INDIANA
Phone 88

1928   JANUARY   1928

RIGHT The January/February page of this 1943 six-page calendar is typical in showing a U.S. Army nurse in uniform.

ABOVE This distributor calendar is similar to the regular Coca-Cola calendar produced for 1928. The only differences are that it bears the name of the retailer, D. H. Wallace Pharmacy, and is smaller in scale.

advertising, and two screw-in posts which held calendar sheets for each day. All that needed to be replaced from year to year were the calendar pads. High-quality desk calendars were also given to high-volume customers and outstanding employees.

CHAPTER THREE

BOTTLES, GLASSES
AND COOLERS

• • • •

The earliest bottles used for Coca-Cola contained only the syrup, not the carbonated beverage. John Pemberton, who invented Coca-Cola, used plain bottles with paper labels marked "Coca-Cola Syrup and Extract" to distribute the syrup to soda fountains, where the syrup was first mixed with plain water and later with carbonated water. Then in 1894 Joseph A. Biedenharn put the carbonated beverage in bottles. These thick-walled, six-ounce bottles used Hutchinson stoppers and were not marked with the Coca-Cola trademark. In 1897, the second bottler to put carbonated Coca-Cola in bottles was the Valdosta (Georgia) Bottling Works owned by R. H. Holmes and E. R. Barber.

In 1899, Benjamin F. Thomas and Joseph B. Whitehead, were given exclusive rights to bottle Coca-Cola in the entire United States except for the territories covered by pre-existing contracts. The first bottles marked "Coca-Cola" to be used in this new business enterprise were Hutchinson-stopper bottles, but within two years crown-top bottles became standard.

LEFT These clear and amber bottles were used between 1905 and 1920. Some bottlers believed that the amber bottles were more effective in preserving the flavor of Coca-Cola.

RIGHT The Hutchinson-stopper bottle was opened by pushing down on the wire loop. The loud popping sound made by this action is the origin of the term "soda pop."

Early bottles

Bottles were originally hand-blown. Glass was mixed in relatively small batches, and bottle sizes were not standardized. The result for today's collectors is a seemingly endless variety of bottles, so early bottles are generally separated into two categories: amber bottles, and more transparent bottles including green, blue, aqua, and colorless.

These early crown-top bottles were identified as containing Coca-Cola by one of three indicators. The trademark "Coca-Cola" might be blown into the glass, the bottle cap could be marked with the trademark, or a diamond-shaped paper label printed with the trademark might be glued to the bottle.

Standardization

The Coca-Cola Company finally addressed the need for a standardized bottle for Coca-Cola. B. F. Thomas put it this way: "We need a bottle which a person can recognize as a Coca-Cola bottle when he feels it in the dark." Bottle manufacturers were invited to submit designs,

and in 1916 a choice was made. The winning design was in fact inspired by a line drawing of a cocoa pod (which had been mistaken for a coca bean). The bottle therefore had an exaggerated bulge around the middle. The glass color that was selected was a light shade of green known as "German green" at the time, but now called "Georgia green" in honor of the home state of Coca-Cola.

By 1920, the new standardized "hobbleskirt" bottle was in widespread use throughout the United States. The November 16, 1915, patent date was blown into the glass just below the Coca-Cola trademark. After renewing the bottle patent in 1923 and registering the shape of the bottle as a design patent in 1937, the classic hobbleskirt bottle was finally registered as a trademark in 1960.

Other containers

Beginning in the mid-1950s, containers other than hobbleskirt bottles were introduced. Coca-Cola was first packaged in flat-top cans in 1955, but on a limited basis, for overseas American military personnel. The late 1960s saw the first widespread use of non-returnable bottles, first made of glass and later plastic.

Cartons and cases

At first, bottles of Coca-Cola were transported in traditional 24-bottle wooden cases stenciled with the trademark "Coca-Cola." These cases were used primarily to take the bottles from the bottling plants to the stores, although some bottlers did sell 24-bottle cases directly on to the consumers. In the mid-1920s the six-bottle cardboard carton was introduced. While the cardboard carrier continues to be used to this day, alternative carriers have also been made of wood, metal, and plastic.

LEFT The hobbleskirt bottle was sometimes used as part of a display, as seen here with this German cardboard bottle topper.

BELOW Before the introduction of the cardboard six-pack carton, finely crafted wooden carriers were made to transport Coca-Cola bottles.

CANS

Having first been drunk from glasses as syrup with water added, then carbonated from bottles, Coca-Cola is probably now most familiar in a can. There is a prolif-eration of different containers to be collected and anyone hoping to find every variation and incarnation of the can is indeed facing a daunting task.

BELOW Ever since the late 1960s, most Coca-Cola cans have been made from a mixture of aluminum and steel. Note how this can, which dates from 1994, features the classic hobbleskirt bottle in its design.

ABOVE The first flat-topped Coca-Cola cans were made of steel and were introduced in the United States in 1959. Prior to this they had been shipped to American servicemen in the Pacific in 1955 and to Europe in 1956.

ABOVE The Coca-Cola Company produced cans to be sent to the Olympic Village for the Moscow Olympics. These were never shipped, however, because of President Carter's decision to boycott the competition.

Early glasses

The classic Coca-Cola bottle has long been recognized as one of the most familiar objects in the world. What few realize, however, is that long before that bottle came into existence, the "Coca-Cola glass" had achieved equal recognition. Consumers had come to associate the product with the glass and the glass with the product. Even glasses that were not marked "Coca-Cola" but which had the same shape were typically called "Coca-Cola glasses".

The syrup line

The first definitive proof of special glasses for Coca-Cola dates from 1900, when the company began promoting a "graduated Coca-Cola glass." This glass was a straight-sided glass to which the script Coca-Cola trademark had been added, and were known as "mineral water" glasses. The word "graduated" referred to the line on the glass approximately three-quarters of an inch from the bottom. Since automatic dispensing machines had not yet been invented this line was very important because it indicated the amount of Coca-Cola syrup to be used. This marking became known as the "syrup line."

The size of the glass was also very important since the ratio of syrup to carbonated water had to be correct. Clearly, in addition to advertising Coca-Cola, the glass was important for maintaining quality control. To make certain that the proper glass was available at a price that retailers could afford to use, The Coca-Cola Company purchased huge quantities of the special glasses and made them available at cost price to the retailers.

The company soon introduced a metal holder marked "Coca-Cola" specially made to hold straight-sided glasses. This holder transformed an unmarked glass into a Coca-Cola glass. Collectors should be aware that The Coca-Cola Company reproduced the metal holder in the 1970s.

RIGHT This 1935 large-scale Canadian cardboard cutout shows the familiar bell-shaped glass. Since 1929 this shape has become closely associated with Coca-Cola throughout the entire world.

Later glasses

In 1905, the company introduced a new glass with a small diameter at the base, flaring out to a larger diameter at the rim. Although today's collectors usually refer to these as "flare glasses," at its introduction, this glass was originally called a "bell" glass.

In 1923, the company introduced a new glass with a turned rim, called a "modified flare glass". By 1926, four million modified flare glasses had been sold. The Coca-Cola glass underwent another significant change in 1929 when the turned edge was made more pronounced, giving the glass a distinct bulge about half an inch from the top. This bulge lowered the center of gravity of the glass and made it harder to tip over, and less likely to chip if it did tip. The glass industry called this a "cupped" glass, but today's collectors call it a "bell" glass.

By 1930 the evolution in the shape of the Coca-Cola glass had come to an end. Only one significant change in glasses has taken place since that time. In the spring of 1955, The Coca-Cola Company broke with tradition and began test-marketing twelve-ounce glasses of Coca-Cola at soda fountains in New York and Los Angeles. This successful twelve-ounce glass was followed in 1961 by a sixteen-ounce "Jumbo", which was designed to accommodate a scoop of ice cream for the "Float with Coke" campaign.

syrup line; the word "Drink" may be missing or replaced by the word "Bottle" or "Enjoy"; the trademark notification may be different or may be missing all together; and the glass may be marked with either a small or large "5¢." Non-English versions of Coca-Cola glasses are also highly collectable, as well as those that were created specifically for events sponsored by Coca-Cola.

Fountain dispensers

Fountain dispensing machines marked "Coca-Cola" and "Coke" are popular collector's items today. However, it is only a few collectors who have them in working order because the mechanisms needed to make them function are both bulky and difficult to maintain.

Associated items

Napkins, coasters, and straws marked Coca-Cola – which were often used in conjunction with Coca-Cola glasses – are also popular pieces of memorabilia to collect.

Since the 1960s, fountain glasses have undergone countless changes. Although bell-shaped glasses are still available, other shapes, often with colorful printing portraying cartoon characters or traditional Coca-Cola artwork, are extensively used. The popularity of paper and plastic cups has also changed the fountain glass picture.

Variations

As with any item issued year after year, there are distinct collectable differences within each category of Coca-Cola glasses. They may have a single, double, or broken

Coolers

When the sale of Coca-Cola in bottles first began, it was the responsibility of the retailer to see that the bottles were kept chilled. Most accomplished this by placing the bottles in their stores' ice-boxes, along with the eggs, butter, cheese and meat. Since these other products had to be kept cold to avoid spoilage, and bottles of Coca-Cola did not, keeping the bottles cold was a low priority. The average grocer kept only a few bottles on ice and when they were sold, new ones weren't always replaced immediately. Consequently, when a customer bought a bottle of Coca-Cola, it wasn't always as cold as it should have been.

It didn't take long for some enterprising bottler to work out that if he supplied the grocer with a Coca-Cola cooler, then an ample supply of properly chilled bottles would always be available. Additionally, there was the added advertising that such a cooler would provide. The first coolers made especially for bottled Coca-Cola were believed to have been barrels that had been cut in half to form tubs in which ice and bottles could be kept. Advertising was added by stenciling or metal signs. Placed in a conspicuous location, this combination of ice and bottles practically begged a customer to have an ice-cold bottle of Coca-Cola, especially on a hot day. Such a half-barrel tub is an example of a "wet cooler," where

ABOVE Early Coca-Cola coolers chilled the bottles by immersing them in ice water. A paper sleeve was therefore used to soak up any excess moisture.

melting ice rather than electricity provides the cooling. With the increasing popularity of bottled Coca-Cola, numerous bottlers devised more successful wet coolers which were nothing more than wooden boxes on legs. A sliding or hinged lid along with a metal lining completed the design. More often than not, the outer wooden case was painted with what later became called "Coca-Cola yellow," with stenciled advertising in "Coca-Cola red."

The next advance in cooler manufacturing in the mid-1920s replaced the wooden exterior with one made of sheet metal. Additional design features included

BELOW This salesman's sample cooler was produced in 1939 as part of the "Business Builders" cooler sales contest. This was five years after the original redesign of the Coca-Cola cooler.

ABOVE *Coca-Cola salesmen had to sell coolers to retailers and therefore used miniature versions such as this to demonstrate the features. This saved them having to transport a full-sized model around with them.*

duced in 1929. Glascock coolers were sold, rather than given, to retailers. Because of the Glascock cooler's superior insulation, the savings on the cost of ice enabled the retailer to recoup the cost of the cooler in less than a year. Unlike many of its predecessors, many examples of the Glascock cooler have survived today.

Although immensely popular, the Glascock cooler was replaced in 1934 by a new cooler with rounded corners. Westinghouse was the exclusive manufacturer the first year, and the Cavalier Corporation began making them as well the following year. Prior to World War II, nearly all the coolers used for Coca-Cola were ice-cooled. Although electric coolers had been available from Glascock as early as 1930, few were sold because they cost approximately ten times

BELOW The red cooler often appeared in advertising, as on this cardboard cutout, so that customers would recognize it when they saw it.

mechanisms that required customers to insert a warm bottle of soda in order to remove a cold bottle and coin-operated mechanisms that permitted the customer to get only one bottle of soda for a nickel. Both innovations made the operation of these coolers more automatic and less trouble to the store owner.

As part of their standardization efforts in 1928, The Coca-Cola Company decided that uniformity was essential. After comparing all the popular coolers in use at the time, a prototype was developed by the company. The Glascock Brothers Manufacturing Company of Muncie, Indiana made the new cooler, which was intro-

as much as wet coolers. In 1945, the company introduced a new streamlined cooler conceived by industrial
designer Raymond Loewy. Loewy's award-winning
design featured an enclosed base concealing the
refrigeration unit.

*BELOW This
folder, in the shape
of the 1941
cooler, advertised
the coin-controlled
mechanism made
by the Vendo
Company.*

Vertical vending machines appeared in the late 1940s.
The machine now handled the entire transaction. The
vending machines produced after 1950 form a bewil-
dering array of shapes, uses, and manufacturers. While
few collectors have the space for coolers and vending
machines, there are numerous associated collectables
such as miniature salesman samples, brochures, and
assorted novelties that are highly prized.

*RIGHT Made by
the Cavalier
Corporation and
able to dispense
51 bottles, this
1951 vending
machine was
called the "C-51."*

CHAPTER FOUR

SIGNS AND TRAYS

• • • •

Coca-Cola has always invested a large percentage of its advertising budget in signs. Those made of cloth, paper, and cardboard were less expensive to produce, less durable, and were meant to be replaced fairly often. However, those made of metal, glass and wood cost more initially, but were intended to last for longer.

Cloth signs

Signs made of oilcloth (weatherproofed canvas) were among the earliest ones used to advertise Coca-Cola. They were pinned to awnings over the entrances to soda fountains and stores where Coca-Cola was sold. Lighter weight muslin signs were also produced for

BELOW From 1923 the company provided free 24-sheet billboards if the bottlers paid for advertising space.

Coca-Cola was advertised on more billboards than any other product. Of course, once a billboard had been pasted into position, it was then lost to collectors, although a few unused billboards do survive. Booklets, photos, and postcards showing the billboard advertisements are more collectable.

occasions such as fairs, ball games, and circuses. Because usually they were meant to be seen at a distance, most cloth signs were large and had limited graphics. More detailed canvas signs were used on Coca-Cola trucks to advertise company-sponsored radio and television shows in the 1940s and 1950s.

Paper signs

Paper signs advertising Coca-Cola have taken several forms: posters or hangers, window strips, and billboards. From the 1890s through the early 1900s, the artwork frequently matched that used on the company's calendars. Later examples showed a variety of different artworks including movie stars, food, and Christmas themes. Some signs were simply tacked to walls, while others (called hangers) had metal strips on the top and bottom edges and a loop for hanging. A paper window strip was designed to be affixed to the inside of a store window with the printed side facing outward. Because such signs faded quickly in bright sunlight, they were intended for short-term use.

In 1923, The Coca-Cola Company began creating 24-sheet posters that when assembled produced a billboard. By 1945, the company could boast that

Cardboard Signs

Cardboard signs with collapsible cardboard easels on the back could be used as freestanding displays or wall signs. Some of the most eye-catching of all Coca-Cola advertising was made of die-cut cardboard displays.

pared artwork showing Coca-Cola in a variety of everyday situations. Since Coca-Cola advertising was changed several times a year, a retailer could be left with walls riddled with holes from hanging signs. Increasing competition for wall space also meant that the Coca-Cola sign might be removed and replaced by one for another product. In 1938 the company introduced corrugated cardboard frames into which cardboard signs could be inserted, securing a permanent location for Coca-Cola advertising.

In 1941 the company replaced the cardboard frames with ones made of wood and metal finished in a metallic gold. The cardboard inserts were changed every

LEFT During the war, women in Coca-Cola advertising were often depicted in uniform. This 1942 cardboard sign shows an Army Nurse.

Among the earliest rectangular cardboard signs used to advertise Coca-Cola were ones placed in streetcars. During the first two decades of the century, when 90 per cent of a city's adult population rode on streetcars, the company spent nearly one-sixth of its advertising budget on streetcar signs. Later these signs were used on other forms of public transportation.

Other rectangular signs came in a range of sizes. Early ones usually featured the artwork used on the company's calendars and trays. Later signs used specially pre-

LEFT Cardboard signs covered in celluloid (an early plastic-like material) are often called celluloid signs even though the printing is on the paper.

January, May, and September. This practice continued into the 1960s, but the wooden and later aluminum frames were no longer marked Coca-Cola.

In addition to rectangular cardboard signs, Coca-Cola has also been advertised with irregular-shaped die-cut cardboard signs, which fall into three main categories: cutouts, festoons, and multipiece displays.

When used by collectors, the term "cutout" usually refers to a single lithographed piece of die-cut cardboard, either freestanding or hanging. Certain general trends are evident in the artwork: soda fountain customers in the 1910s, bathing beauties in the 1920s, movie stars in the 1930s and military personnel in the 1940s. Starting in the mid-1920s, Coca-Cola with food was also a frequent subject. Beginning in 1931, The Coca-Cola Company began issuing Santa Claus cutouts.

A festoon is a set of die-cut cardboard signs designed to hang as a unit from a wall or soda fountain backbar. The first festoons were nothing more

than a series of letters strung together to spell out "Coca-Cola", but they soon became more colorful and decorative affairs.

In an attempt to dominate storefront windows, The Coca-Cola Company devised multi-piece sets of die-cut cardboard signs capable of spanning an entire window. These could be set up to create a three-dimensional effect. The use of these displays reached their zenith in the period from the late 1920s through the 1930s, when as many as twenty separate pieces were used to create one display.

CUT-OUT SIGNS

Much of Coca-Cola's advertising was seen on cardboard cutout displays. These were erected in soda fountains and in stores where the drink was for sale. Cutouts were often in irregular shapes and as the designs developed they became more elaborate still. Some were embossed or folded in order to give them a three-dimensional appearance, others were made up of many parts, some of which could move independently, bringing the whole display to life.

LEFT This 1924 cardboard cutout shows the Coca-Cola girl for that particular year. During the first few decades of the century, one girl would be featured across the year's range of advertising items. She might appear on calendars, trays, cutouts and other signs.

ABOVE The design of cardboard cutouts became more sophisticated during the 1920s and 1930s. Many were made up of several separate pieces or had working parts, such as the paper parasol on this example.

RIGHT This 1922 folded cardboard cutout shows a young woman wearing a swimsuit typical of the time. She is riding an "aquaplane", a surfboard-like device that was towed by a motorboat.

LEFT This small metal sign is unusual in that the artwork obscures part of the Coca-Cola trademark. Even by 1927, however, the trademark was so well known that anyone seeing the advert would know that it was for Coca-Cola.

with few colors and graphics so they could be read at a distance. By contrast, indoor signs would be seen more closely and for a longer period of time. Consequently they were usually more elaborate in design and used more colors and detailed graphics to convey the message. To justify their higher cost, metal signs were intended to remain in place, whether indoors or out, for a longer period of time than either cloth, paper, or cardboard signs.

Some outdoor signs were made of thin tin-plated metal with a lithographed finish, while others meant for more extended use were made of heavy metal with a porcelain enamel finish. The thin metal signs usually had no holes for hanging and were called "tacker signs" because they were installed by nailing right through the metal to attach them to walls and fences. Porcelain signs came with pre-drilled holes, grommets, or brackets for hanging. Starting in the 1920s, signs were designed with special frames and poles so that they could stand alone

Metal signs

BELOW Two-sided metal arrow signs were hung from wrought-iron brackets, and were attached at right angles to a wall.

Most metal signs were designed exclusively to be used outdoors because of their durability, but some were intended specifically for indoors and others for hanging in either location. Metal signs were manufactured in all sizes, shapes, and designs in order to be used in a variety of places. Outdoor signs tended to be fairly simple

BUVEZ Coca-Cola
TRADE MARK REGISTERED
DÉLICIEUX ET RAFRAÎCHISSANT 5¢

DRINK A Bottle of Carbonated Coca-Cola
5¢   5¢
THE MOST REFRESHING DRINK IN THE WORLD.

outside stores as well as along well-traveled thoroughfares. The company also made two-sided flange signs which attached to buildings at right angles so that potential customers could view the signs from both directions. For some business establishments, the company produced large signs that carried the name of the business in addition to an advertisement for Coca-Cola.

Indoor metal signs were generally smaller than their outdoor equivalents. Many were lithographed in full color to enhance not only the attractiveness of the advertising, but the interior of the store as well. The artwork was frequently pictorial, showing attractive women along with glasses or bottles of Coca-Cola. Many indoor signs were self-framed, meaning that they were formed by stamping the sign and the frame from the same sheet of metal. Because of their eye-catching appeal, these signs usually remained hanging until company representatives came to replace them with the next Coca-Cola advertisement.

ABOVE Bottles with paper labels were used throughout the world. Here they are used on a French metal tacker sign.

LEFT Dating from about 1903, this oval sign may be the first metal sign to feature the straight-sided Coca-Cola bottle with a paper label.

Glass signs

Glass signs were made by printing the advertising message in reverse on the back side of a piece of glass. When viewed from the front, the message showed through the glass correctly. This technique is called reverse painting on glass. The effect of the sparkling clean glass made the sign more vibrant than either a cardboard or a metal sign.

Glass signs with Coca-Cola advertising first appeared around 1900. The earliest known examples are oval or round and carry the "Drink Coca-Cola 5¢" message with no pictorial graphics. They were usually hung by metal chains that were attached to the sign itself. Later, thick, rectangular, beveled glass signs carried the message to "Drink Coca-Cola." In the 1920s, round glass signs were designed to be glued directly to mirrored walls and backbars in drug stores and soda fountains. In the 1930s, Art Deco reverse-painted glass signs were made available for some locations. The use of this type of glass sign ended by the 1950s, replaced by self-contained electric light-up fixtures with glass panels.

Wooden signs

Beginning in 1933 and continuing into the 1950s, wood was used to produce wooden signs for indoor use. The wood used was actually plywood or board made from compressed wood fibers.

In fact, most of these signs were not made exclusively of wood, but had embellishments made of other materials including metal, plaster, rope,

RIGHT Kay Displays, Inc made many of Coca-Cola's wood and metal signs. This example is made of plywood with three-dimensional metal trim.

RIGHT An Art Deco sign from 1933. This example combines silver and black reverse-painted glass and wooden embellishments.

cloth, and plastic. These added a three-dimensional quality, thereby increasing the attractiveness of the signs. Virtually all of these signs were made by the advertising firm Kay Displays, Inc. Because of their extensive variety and good quality, the signs produced by this company form a fascinating collection in their own right.

In addition to Kay Displays' signs, board was also used for outdoor signs during World War II. Because of the war effort, metal was in short supply, and board served as a temporary replacement. There are a number of instances where the artwork used on board signs was the same as that previously used on metal signs.

Utilitarian signs

Coca-Cola advertising served a secondary purpose on some signs. The primary purposes were as thermometers, menu boards, chalkboards, "Push" and "Pull" door signs, and door push bars.

Thermometers were manufactured in wood well into the 1920s, then in metal starting in the 1920s, in board during World War II, and finally in plastic starting in the 1960s. Wall-mounted menu boards were manufactured by Kay Displays, primarily of wood. Strips preprinted with food choices and prices could be slotted into existing channels. Chalkboards, made of cardboard or metal, served the same purpose as menu boards, but allowed the daily "specials" to be changed easily. Door signs were a familiar sight, reminding patrons of Coca-Cola as they entered stores and restaurants where they might order a drink of Coca-Cola.

RIGHT Art Deco in its styling and practical in its function, this metal thermometer would have been hung in an up-to-date drug store or soda fountain during the 1940s. It actually dates from 1941.

41

Trays

The "Coca-Cola tray." is perhaps the item most closely associated with Coca-Cola advertising. Beginning in the 1890s and continuing to this day, a series of metal trays has carried the "Drink Coca-Cola" message. The enduring qualities of metal, combined with the relatively large number that were produced, have guaranteed the survival of many trays.

Coca-Cola trays can be divided into three general categories depending on their intended use: serving trays, change trays, and TV trays. Although they were frequently used as coasters and ashtrays, change trays were supposed to be used to return change to customers after they had paid their bills. Since many customers left a gratuity on these trays, they are often known as "tip trays."

ABOVE The new straight-sided, paper-label Coca-Cola bottle was first used in advertising on metal "Bottle Trays" such as the one shown above.

The advertising novelty business, which included the manufacture of trays, is said to have started in Coshocton, Ohio. In 1887, J. F. Meek, the publisher of a Coshocton newspaper, established a company, called the Tuscarora Advertising Company, to handle his growing business.

ABOVE AND BELOW The "Hamilton King Girl" rectangular serving tray was accompanied by the matching oval change tray, or tip tray. Both items were made of metal and were first produced in 1910.

H. D. Beach, another Coshocton publisher, started his own novelty business in 1888 under the name of the Standard Advertising Company, and in 1900 the two businessmen merged their businesses into one calling it the Meek and Beach Company. Beach soon decided to sell his interest to Meek and to establish the H. D. Beach Company. Meek then shortened the name of the Meek and Beach Company to the Meek Company, and in 1909, he changed it yet again, this time to American Art Works. It was under that name that the company went on to produce most of the Coca-Cola trays from 1910 to the 1940s.

BELOW The artwork used on this tray also appears on the 1922 calendar. The calendar reveals that the woman is in fact at a baseball game and, for that reason, the tray is commonly known as the "Baseball Girl" tray.

In addition to Coshocton-based companies, the following manufacturers also made Coca-Cola trays: Sentenne & Green (New York), the 1899 trays; Charles W. Shonk Company (Chicago), the 1903 and 1907 trays; the N.Y. Metal Ceiling Company (New York), the 1906 trays; Stelad Signs-Passaic Metal Ware Company (New Jersey), the 1913, 1914, and 1916 trays; and Tindeco (Baltimore), some of the 1927 and 1929 trays.

The earliest known tray featuring Coca-Cola dates from 1897. The shape of American Coca-Cola trays has changed over the years, starting with all round trays before 1903, followed by a mixture of round, oval, and rectangular trays through 1920, and concluding with all rectangular trays from 1921. The series ended with the production of the so-called Pansy trays in the 1960s. After that time, The Coca-Cola Company and others began issuing reproduction trays in many shapes.

A list of the Coshocton firms and the Coca-Cola trays they made in particular years follows: Standard Advertising Company, the 1900 Coca-Cola trays; The Meek and Beach Company, some of the 1901 Coca-Cola trays; The Meek Company, the remainder of the 1901 Coca-Cola trays, as well as the 1905 Coca-Cola trays; The H. D. Beach Company, the 1909 and 1922 Coca-Cola trays; and American Art Works, the 1910 trays and the majority of the trays produced from 1923 to 1942 inclusive.

Exactly how many of the early trays were produced is not known. Before the turn of the century, however, it is known that a tray manufacturer would make as few as fifty trays for a client. In view of the size of The Coca-Cola Company's advertising

BELOW Round Mexican trays, such as this one that dates from 1959, often showed Latin women going about a variety of everyday activities.

budget at the time, it is safe to assume that a considerably larger number of trays was produced for the company's use. Records do tell us that by 1913, two million trays, all for fountain use, were being distributed annually. Prior to the late 1920s, most trays showed a glass rather than a bottle. After 1930, all standard trays showed a bottle.

As the company ordered trays in such large quantities, the cost of an individual tray was kept to a minimum. Turn-of-the-century trays cost approximately 30¢ each, while those throughout the 1920s and 1930s cost between 12¢ and 15¢ each. Between World War 11 and the 1960s, the price ranged from 24¢ to 45¢ each.

A few examples of Coca-Cola trays were produced for foreign markets as early as the 1920s, but most of the foreign trays date from after World War 11. Numerous trays were produced for use in Mexico and Canada.

In the 1920s, the company began advertising Coca-Cola as being good with food. They therefore produced sandwich plates and other china depicting the Coca-Cola bottle and glass. Ceramic, glass, Bakelite, metal, and plastic ashtrays carrying the Coca-Cola logo were also introduced.

BELOW Baseball has long been associated with Coca-Cola and here it is represented on a 1950s ashtray. A Coca-Cola ashtray on the table meant that the product was always on the mind when ordering the next drink.

CHAPTER FIVE

CLOCKS

● ● ● ●

Clocks are one of the more expensive but enduring forms of advertising used for Coca-Cola. As early as the 1890s, The Coca-Cola Company saw the value of producing permanent advertising that promoted the sale of their product. While most other advertising was expected to last for less than a year, clocks were designed to last indefinitely, thereby justifying their higher initial cost.

The Baird Clock Company of Plattsburgh, New York was the first company to make Coca-Cola clocks. First used in 1893, each clock cost the company $2.75 and was given as a premium to dealers who bought fifty gallons of Coca-Cola syrup in a single year. Baird clocks, key-wound and pendulum-driven, had large round faces with Roman numerals. Frequently called a "figure-eight" clock, the standard Baird clock had two round doors — one positioned over the face and the other over the pendulum — that were made of molded composition, a combination of sawdust, wood fibers, and glue. The raised lettering on the surface of the upper door carried the advertising slogan, "Coca-Cola, The Ideal Brain Tonic," that was used from 1893 through to 1897. The slogans on the smaller lower door varied over the years and

LEFT Kay Designs, Inc. produced this deluxe clock with ornamental rings and a wide background panel for high-quality establishments.

RIGHT Despite being made nearly a century ago, many schoolhouse clocks, such as the example here, still work today. Note the ornate woodwork and the glass door over the pendulum compartment. This clock was made by the Welch Manufacturing Company.

RIGHT "Figure-eight" Baird clocks were usually refinished when they started to show signs of wear. This does not appear to have happened to this particular example, however, which dates from about 1895.

included such phrases as "Delightful Beverage," "Specific for Headache," "Relieves Mental & Physical Exhaustion," "5¢," "Relieves Exhaustion," "Delicious," and "Refreshing." Baird also made "gallery" versions of these "Brain Tonic" clocks that were round, but did not have the pendulum or lower door portion. A later Baird clock carried the advertising on metal panel inserts. Even though a remarkable number of these clocks from the 1890s have survived, they have always been highly sought after and are therefore expensive to acquire. Collectors should be aware that these early clocks have been reproduced in more recent times.

The schoolhouse clock was the next type of clock used to advertise Coca-Cola. The upper portion was octagonal in shape and made of finished wood surrounding a glass-covered, circular face. The lower portion consisted of a wood and glass door covering a compartment for the pendulum. Unlike a Baird clock, the advertising message was printed on a schoolhouse clock's face in red. Occasionally these clocks are found with Coca-Cola artwork, lithographed on cardboard, inserted in the case behind the pendulum. Schoolhouse clocks advertising Coca-Cola were made first by the Welch Manufacturing Company around the turn of the century and later by the Ingraham Company.

In about 1905, The Coca-Cola Company began distributing large rectangular clocks, commonly called regulator clocks. This type of clock had a wooden case with a single door consisting of two framed pieces of glass. Once again, the face carried the advertising for Coca-Cola printed in red. Using the same face as on the earlier schoolhouse clocks, Ingraham produced this kind of clock through 1910. Beginning in 1911, The Coca-Cola Company turned to the Gilbert Clock Corporation to produce regulators. Several changes were made at this point: the advertising on the face was simplified to "Drink Coca-Cola," the numerals were changed from Roman to Arabic, and advertising was added to the lower glass panel. These rectangular clocks were available through the 1930s, but were gradually replaced by electric clocks. Until these clocks were discontinued in 1941, Gilbert made many changes to the wooden case as well as the advertising message.

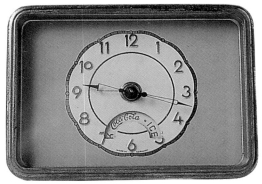

BELOW The main feature of this wind-up clock dating from about 1935 is the "Drink Coca-Cola • Ice Cold" slogan.

This rotates within the semicircular window at the bottom of dial when the clock is running.

ABOVE From 1905 to 1915, leather, wind-up clocks such as this were widely distributed. This example is decorated with gold-leaf lettering.

47

Electric clocks advertising Coca-Cola began to appear in the early 1930s. They were suitable for more locations because they were smaller and didn't need to be wound. The advertising usually appeared either on the face of the clock or on the glass covering the face. At first the cases were made of wood and metal. Plastic cases and faces began to appear in the late 1950s. Starting in the late 1930s, some clocks were illuminated with either neon or ordinary light bulbs.

After World War II, as electric clocks became less expensive, clocks were used much more extensively to advertise Coca-Cola. As a result, there are many styles and variations of clocks, made by dozens of different manufacturers. The slogans and graphics, as well as the materials and design, are helpful to collectors when they are trying to date these clocks.

In addition to these wall clocks, The Coca-Cola Company and its local bottlers also distributed table and desk clocks. Among the earliest of these, dating from around 1910, are clocks with leather-covered cases. The advertising appeared in gold-stamped lettering on the cases rather than on the clock itself. Later table clocks included glass-domed anniversary clocks and smaller brass-cased clocks, with animated advertising.

ABOVE The woman illustrated on this clock is reminiscent of the artwork of Charles Dana Gibson. The clock is therefore called the "Gibson Girl" clock.

ABOVE The plastic case of this clock is illuminated from within by a ring-shaped fluorescent bulb. The popular "things go better with Coke" logo is prominently displayed over the top left of the dial. The clock dates from about 1963.

BELOW The neon tubing that surrounds the face of this clock illuminates both the clock and the premises on which it is kept, for example a store that stays open into the dark hours of evening and night.

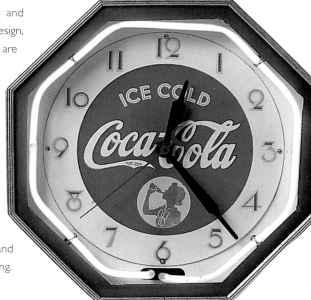

48

EDUCATIONAL ITEMS
AND TOYS

• • • •

When Coca-Cola was first sold, it was advertised as being the perfect tonic for the work-weary. As a result of its claims to almost medicinal qualities, it was generally understood that Coca-Cola was an adult drink. Because of the high caffeine content (which was nearly three times what it is now), combined with persistent, but erroneous, rumors about alcohol and cocaine, some mothers even forbade their children to drink it. For its part, The Coca-Cola Company did not try to appeal to children during its earlier years. With the passage of the Pure Food and Drug Act in 1906 and the reduction of the caffeine content in the late 1910s, The Coca-Cola Company began appealing to the youth market during the 1920s.

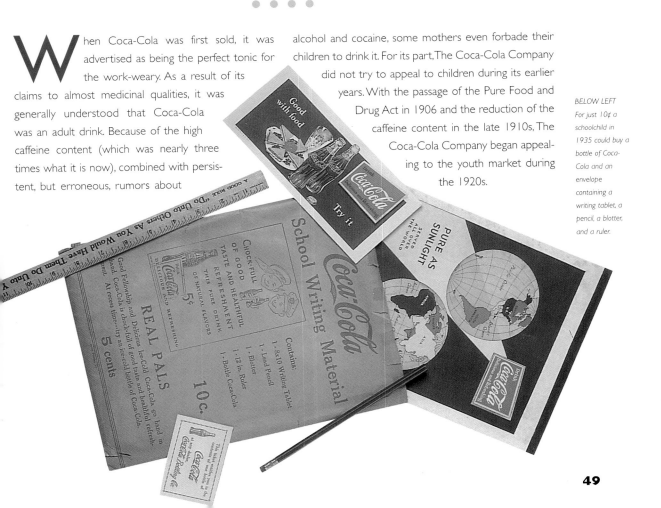

BELOW LEFT
For just 10¢ a schoolchild in 1935 could buy a bottle of Coca-Cola and an envelope containing a writing tablet, a pencil, a blotter, and a ruler.

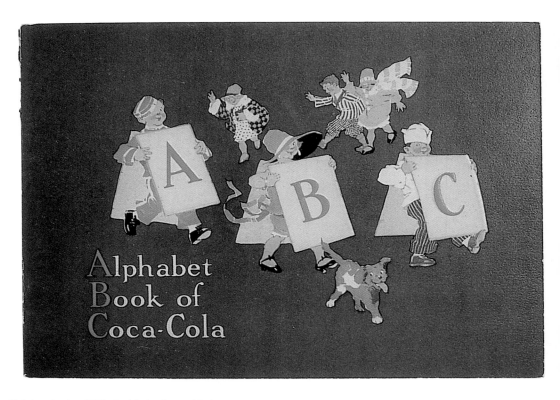

Children in the 1920s had little disposable income with which to buy Coca-Cola, so there would have been little point appealing to them directly. What the company and its bottlers did instead was use the educational system to reach children. At first they approached teachers, principals, and superintendents, rather than contacting schoolchildren directly. Educators were invited to take tours of bottling plants, and they were sent free booklets telling them how safe and wholesome Coca-Cola was. Many bottlers donated useful items to schools in their areas: Coca-Cola pencils, blotters, and calendars were the most popular giveaways. Many bottlers also donated Coca-Cola clocks.

At the 1923 "Sales and Advertising Conference of the Bottlers of Coca-Cola," it was openly suggested for the first time that advertising efforts be directed specifically toward children. Roy Booker, a spokesman for an advertising novelties company, proposed that bottlers "give each child a ruler, a pencil and three blotters." Following Booker's presentation, the company began producing a special ruler imprinted with the words, "Do Unto Others As You Would Have Them Do Unto You." This Golden Rule ruler had possibly the longest life of any Coca-Cola advertising item — remaining virtually unchanged for over 45 years.

The list of Coca-Cola advertising materials given away free to schoolchildren soon expanded to include erasers, tablets, book covers, pens, maps, and printed schedules for school athletic events. In the late 1920s and 1930s, "Nature Study" cards described the natural world; in the early 1930s, "Famous Doctors" folders detailed medical advancements over the centuries; in the 1940s and 1950s, "Our America" kits described major American industries; in the late 1950s and early 1960s, "Elementary Science Laboratory" kits enabled students to conduct their own modest scientific experiments; and in the late 1960s, "Golden Legacy" comic books told the history of famous black Americans. The "Black Guardians of Freedom" section of the Golden Legacy series included an excerpt from Martin Luther King Jr.'s "I Have a Dream" speech.

Because they were given out in such large quantities, these items are easy to collect today, but as similar pieces

were distributed over several decades, they can be difficult to date. The slogans on these items can be used to pinpoint the years of use. For example, "Pure As Sunlight" was used in the late 1920s and early 1930s; "A Pure Drink of Natural Flavors" was used in the 1930s: "Coke = Coca-Cola" was used in the 1940s and 1950s: "It's the real thing" appeared in the 1960s; and "Have a Coke and smile" and "Coke is it!" in the 1970s. Some slogans, such as "Drink Coca-Cola in Bottles" and "Have a Coke" were used year after year, making it is nearly impossible to date examples exactly.

LEFT Before the advent of ballpoint pens, every pupil would have had an inkwell such as this on their desk in order to refill their fountain pen.

BELOW The style of artwork seen on this blotter from 1927 is typical of that used in Coca-Cola advertising during the later half of the 1920s.

CARDS

Various games have been produced featuring Coca-Cola advertising, such as darts, dominoes, bingo and checkers. Playing cards lend themselves to advertising, however, with the opportunity to repeat artwork on the reverse of each card. Designs used have included the Coca-Cola girl from the annual calendars and, during wartime, both men and women in uniform.

LEFT These playing cards were made in about 1940 by the Atlantic Playing Card Company. They feature the well-known "Silhouette Girl" artwork on the reverse of each card.

RIGHT The Western Coca-Cola Bottling Company sold this pack of playing cards for 25¢. They featured the "Elaine" artwork, which also featured on the 1915 Coca-Cola calendar.

Toys and games

For some enthusiasts, toys and games are the most beloved of all Coca-Cola collectables. Until the company instituted a licensing program in the 1980s, toy manufacturers in many countries produced countless toys with the Coca-Cola trademark, but without the company's involvement. However, the company has produced such things as playing cards and games to promote the sale of Coca-Cola.

In the days before customers paid a deposit on bottles, bottlers needed some method to encourage the return of empty bottles. Some local bottlers developed plans to accomplish this goal. When customers returned empty bottles to stores, they were given coupons indicating the number of bottles they had returned. After collecting a sufficient number of coupons, the customer could then visit the bottler and exchange the coupons for useful "gifts." These were usually nothing more than readily available household items. Other bottlers, in an obvious effort to increase sales, merely offered the same premiums in exchange for bottle caps. In both cases, among the most popular of these gifts were mass-produced toys to which the bottlers simply added the Coca-Cola logo.

The Coca-Cola bottler in St. Louis, Missouri, probably led all others in the distribution of these toys in the 1920s and 1930s. Vintage photographs of his special premium room show scooters, bicycles, dolls,

ABOVE The Metalcraft Corporation of St. Louis, Missouri made this miniature truck. It could be bought in department stores or by mail order.

LEFT This shows the roof of the key-wound American flyer train. Each car of the train advertised Coca-Cola on its roof. The train dates from the 1930s.

ABOVE The bottler in St. Louis, Missouri, probably ordered this train to be made by The Metal Corporation. He would have then exchanged it for customers' Coca-Cola coupons.

play stoves, wagons and lanterns. It is probably not a coincidence that the first Coca-Cola toy trucks were manufactured by The Metalcraft Corporation, which is also located in St. Louis.

ABOVE A miniature Coca-Cola bottle is dispensed from this replica Vendo V-83 machine when a coin is inserted. This toy bank was made in about 1948.

In the first three decades of the century, Coca-Cola bottlers sporadically distributed playing cards featuring the same artwork used on other items. In the 1930s and 1940s, the company and its bottlers took advantage of the card-playing craze then sweeping the nation by distributing numerous decks of playing cards advertising Coca-Cola, and distributing Coca-Cola playing cards has been a standard advertising practice since that time. While collectors prefer complete decks in original boxes, some decks are so difficult to obtain in this form that collectors will sometimes settle for finding a single card.

From the early 1940s and continuing into the 1960s, the Coca-Cola company

RIGHT This cardboard whistle features the straight-sided, paper-label bottle. The whistle makes a high-pitched sound when blown.

produced a series of games, manufactured by the Milton Bradley Company of Springfield, Massachusetts. These games were usually packaged in red boxes. The list of games produced includes anagrams, backgammon, bingo, checkers, chess, cribbage, darts, dominoes, ring toss, tic-tac-toe, and wall quoits. These games were typically distributed to schools, churches, clubs, and hospi-

tals. During World War II, the company and the bottlers also distributed these games to military bases both in the United States and abroad.

Miniatures, small-sized replicas of larger items, are also covered in the category of toys. For Coca-Cola, miniatures included bottles, cartons, cases, coolers.

whistles. Since most of these toys were produced without the knowledge or permission of The Coca-Cola Company, there is little information about exactly what was produced and when. For this reason, perhaps no other area of Coca-Cola collecting is as exciting as this one, since previously unknown toys are constantly being discovered.

dispensers, and glasses. It was not surprising that The Coca-Cola Company distributed miniature versions of its own merchandising items, thereby enabling children to play at being Coca-Cola customers and dealers. Toy manufacturers have also made toy coolers and dispensers, some of which double as savings banks.

ABOVE The "Tower of Hanoi" game involved moving the eight circular disks from one peg to another by carefully following a set of rules.

BELOW Gull-wing trucks were used by many Coca-Cola bottlers during the late 1940s. This plastic model made by Louis Marx & Company of New York is a fairly faithful representation.

Toys and games form such an eclectic group of objects that it is difficult to generalize about them. Toy trucks and other vehicles traditionally form the foundation for most collections of Coca-Cola toys. The list of Coca-Cola toys is a seemingly endless one and includes bang guns, clickers, jump ropes, kites, marbles, puzzles, spinning tops, toy aircraft, toy robots, and

CHAPTER SEVEN

NOVELTIES AND MISCELLANEOUS ITEMS

● ● ● ●

One of the most popular, personal, and yet inexpensive forms of advertising for Coca-Cola has been novelties. Records show, for example, that from 1906 to 1913, the company made the following expenditures for novelties: more than $90,000 for leather novelties; $30,000 for celluloid novelties; $25,000 for matches; $15,000 for pocketknives; $30,000 for watch fobs; and $40,000 for fans.

Leather novelties included wallets, coin purses, match safes, and pocket notebooks. The advertising that appeared on the leather was usually imprinted using gold leaf. Wallets and coin purses were issued from early in the century.

Before safety matches, a match safe was used in order to enclose a book of matches so that they wouldn't accidentally ignite while in a pocket.

In addition to having blank pages for making personal notes, leather-covered notebooks advertising Coca-Cola usually carried a listing of how much syrup each retailer had used during the previous year.

Made from cellulose (a wood fiber derivative), celluloid was an early forerunner of plastic. A thin sheet of transparent celluloid could be used to cover the paper portion of an

RIGHT This leather match safe commemorates the National Association of Retail Druggists (NARD) trade convention in 1906.

LEFT Store clerks were usually given more expensive novelties such as this leather coin purse in order to build and protect product loyalty. Note the gold-leaf stamping.

RIGHT This pocket mirror is unusual in that the artwork only appears elsewhere in a magazine ad; it was usually copied from the year's calendar.

BELOW Before 1916 company-issued pocket mirrors only promoted fountain Coca-Cola. Some bottlers produced their own mirrors.

advertising item printed in full color, thereby increasing that item's durability. Additionally, advertising objects could be made from non-transparent celluloid by printing directly on the celluloid itself. Celluloid-covered items included signs, pocket mirrors, watch fobs, and cuff links, while items made entirely of celluloid included bookmarks, pocketknife handles, and covers for pocket notebooks, stamp holders and blotter pads.

Match books

The use of book matches to advertise Coca-Cola seems to have begun shortly after the turn of the century. Since match books were disposable items, relatively few examples were saved. Those that have survived testify to the wide variety of cover designs that were used in the early years. In addition to the advertising on the cover, it was not unusual for early match books to have advertising slogans on each individual match. Before World War I, several different

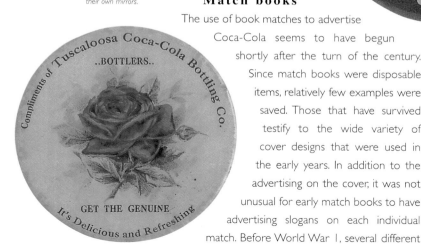

designs were used each year. After that time the company employed fewer designs, often using the same artwork for several years in a row. Since the late 1920s, bottlers have frequently shared the cover advertising space with local businesses that sold Coca-Cola. Matches were also made to commemorate events such as company anniversaries and world's fairs.

Pocketknives

Pocketknives have also been a popular Coca-Cola giveaway since the turn of the century. In addition to the blades, some pocketknives also had bottle openers and corkscrews. Most Coca-Cola pocketknives were distributed by local bottlers, some of whom added their name to the Coca-Cola advertising.

Pocket watches

Made of celluloid or metal, or a combination of both, a watch fob was attached by a leather strap to a pocket watch. The fob hung out of the pocket so that a pull on the fob would bring out the watch. Although there are many different examples of watch fobs advertising Coca-Cola, they were only used for a relatively short period beginning in about 1905. The increasing popularity of wrist watches reduced the necessity for watch fobs, and they were eventually phased out.

Fans

The earliest known fans date from the 1890s. They were made of cardboard with attached wooden handles. From the late 1890s and well into the 1910s, the company used "Japanese" rice paper fans with bamboo handles. After that time, cardboard fans were distributed. Fans were given away to individuals, as well as to churches and other civic organizations. Their value as an advertising device is at once clear. What better time to remind someone of the cooling effects of ice-cold Coca-Cola than during the heat of a hot summer? One of the few sets of remaining records to mention such quantities indicates that in 1913 alone a staggering one million fans were given away to customers.

Bottle openers

Perhaps the most enduring of all novelties, bottle openers were

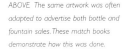

ABOVE The same artwork was often adapted to advertise both bottle and fountain sales. These match books demonstrate how this was done.

very nearly indestructible. Usually stamped from a flat sheet of metal, they were easily and cheaply produced. Because individual bottlers usually arranged for the manufacture of openers, there are countless different examples available to collectors.

In addition to those novelties already mentioned, ice picks, fly swatters, key rings, thimbles, salt and pepper shakers, cigarette lighters, mechanical pencils, pens, ashtrays, scorekeepers, sheet music, jewelry, advertising buttons, and sewing kits have all been used at one time or another in order to promote Coca-Cola. Novelties were distributed to consumers by door-to-door canvassing, through mass mailings, as souvenirs of bottling plant tours, for redemption of bottle caps, and by mail-in offers, to name but a few of the many methods employed.

LEFT This hand-shaped, lithographed metal spinner could be used to determine who paid for the next drink in a soda fountain.

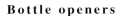

BELOW Sandwiches could be marked with the Coca-Cola trademark by placing them in this electric toaster. What better way to suggest to customers that they might want a Coca-Cola with their meal?

RIGHT Brass door knobs with the Coca-Cola trademark were used in company branch offices throughout the United States. The example shown here is from the Candler Building in Baltimore, Maryland.

Other collectables

Some Coca-Cola collectors concentrate on items that were used to conduct the mundane business of manufacturing, distributing, and selling Coca-Cola. Others search out special awards and trophies, while others still prize those advertising specialties offered only once, or at most a few times. Finally, some collectors devote their time to items that were not produced by The Coca-Cola Company or its bottlers, but which nevertheless show advertising for Coca-Cola.

Stationery, invoices, receipts, and checks carrying the Coca-Cola trademark, ordinary building hardware, such as doorknobs and padlocks, marked with the Coca-Cola logo, are all collectable.

To honor significant achievements, businesses have traditionally given awards to their employees. The Coca-Cola Company gave jewelry to employees to recognize such achievements as the number of years of employment, safe driving, and retirement. In addition, they presented plaques and awards to individual bottlers in order to acknowledge high sales figures or to celebrate bottlers' anniversaries.

Over the years, in an effort to increase their own business, manufacturers of advertising items have presented the company and its bottlers with new ideas for promoting Coca-Cola. Some of the resulting items were adopted and issued over long periods of time, while others were tried for a year or two and then discontin-

ued because of their expense or inferior design. This group of short-lived items includes some of the most desirable of all Coca-Cola collectables.

Not only has the Coca-Cola trademark been used to promote the sale of Coca-Cola, it has also been used by other firms to advertise their own products. Many manufacturers of advertising material have used Coca-Cola items made by them as exemplars of the quality of their work. For example, advertisements for sign makers often showed a Coca-Cola sign among others, and truck manufacturers frequently pictured Coca-Cola trucks in their advertising. Vintage picture postcards and photographs showing Coca-Cola items also fall into this category.

BELOW When a match was pulled from the holder on top of the bottle on this ashtray, it was automatically ignited. The ashtray is therefore called a "Pullmatch."

LEFT The Hackney Wagon Company of North Carolina made these benches to be used in front of stores where bottled Coca-Cola was sold.

New collectables

The 1970s saw The Coca-Cola Company's first real interest in the memorabilia craze that had begun sweeping the nation. The company offered reproductions of early trays, calendars, glasses, and other items to a nostalgia-hungry public. The ensuing interest generated by these reproductions is largely responsible for launching the memorabilia-collecting phenomenon which continues to this day. All this collecting activity also attracted unscrupulous individuals who, without the permission of The Coca-Cola Company, produced fake advertising pieces marked with the Coca-Cola trademark and the wholesale manufacture of large quantities of illegal collectables flourished during the 1970s. Long after these bogus items were produced, they continue to cause problems for novice and experienced collectors alike.

Reproductions

Technically speaking, a reproduction is a copy of an older item. A casual observer may not notice any difference between the two, but a knowledgeable collector will always be able to detect differences between the original and the reproduction. For example, today's printing processes are different from those that were used at the turn of the century. The quality of workmanship is rarely as good on a reproduction as on an original. There are often subtle variations in size, color, and material. If a collector can place a reproduction and its original counterpart side by side, the differences are usually strikingly obvious.

LEFT AND RIGHT These fantasy pocketknives are often found for sale. They are easily mass-produced and as a result are fairly common.

Fantasy items

A fantasy item is one that appears to be old, but is not. Unlike a reproduction, a fantasy item has no original counterpart. To give them an air of authenticity, most fantasy items incorporate old artwork and slogans. Some include bogus dates, manufacturers, and events.

Over the years, these fantasy items have included brass belt buckles, metal free-drink tokens, so-called pub mirrors, trays, pocket mirrors, money clips, paperweights, pocketknives, playing cards, glassware, signs, watch fobs, and pin-back buttons. Other fantasy items have been created by taking truly old, unmarked items and adding the Coca-Cola trademark. These items are therefore somewhat harder to detect. The list of these items includes pocketknives, pocket watches, watch fobs, bone-handled eating utensils, celluloid dresser sets, glass doorknobs, and straight razors.

Licensed items

In the mid-1980s, The Coca-Cola Company established a licensing program whereby they sanctioned the manufacture of items bearing the Coca-Cola trademark. Although many such items feature old Coca-Cola advertising artwork, they do not pretend to be genuinely old. Licensed items include clothing, towels, rugs, watches, playing cards, postcards, trays, glassware, pins, napkin and straw dispensers, commemorative bottles, Christmas ornaments, calendars, limited edition prints, puzzles, canisters, and thermometers.

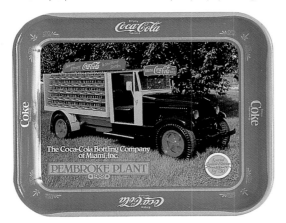

LEFT Some manufacturers claim that their recently produced items are limited editions in order to enhance their value to collectors of memorabilia.

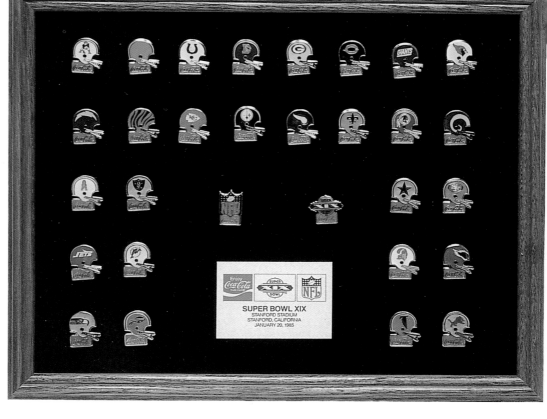

There are, in fact, nearly as many reproduction, fantasy, and licensed items as there are old surviving collectables. New items are being produced at an ever-increasing rate. It is impossible to devise a set of rules that will permit collectors to infallibly recognize what is authentically old and what is not. However, there are a few strategies to guide collectors. First, the more authentic Coca-Cola collectables a collector sees personally, the less likely he or she will be deceived by reproductions and fantasy items. Get to know other collectors and take the opportunity to study their collections. Antique advertising shows, auctions, museums, and collectors' conventions are not only excellent places to meet other collectors, but to examine original items as well.

There are also numerous reference books and price guides which picture Coca-Cola collectables and provide additional descriptions and information.